I Can Read

Teacher's Choice Series

Robin W. Holland
Columbus, Ohio

Illustrations by
Steve Pileggi

Dominie Press, Inc.

The development of the *Teacher's Choice Series* was supported by the Reading Recovery project at California State University, San Bernardino. All authors' royalties from the sale of the *Teacher's Choice Series* will be used to support various Reading Recovery projects.

Publisher: Raymond Yuen
Series Editor: Stanley L. Swartz
Illustrator: Steve Pileggi
Cover Designer: Steve Morris
Page Design: Pamela S. Pettigrew

Published by:

Dominie Press, Inc.

1949 Kellogg Avenue
Carlsbad, California 92008 USA

ISBN 1-56270-547-4
Printed in Singapore by PH Productions.
2 3 4 5 6 PH 99 98 97

I can read at school.

I can read at home.

I can read at the park.

I can read at the store.

I can read at the pool.

I can read at the corner.

I can read everywhere!

About the Author

Robin Holland received a B.S. in Elementary Education in 1974 and an M.A. in Developmental Reading in 1975 from The Ohio State University. She is currently a Reading Recovery™ Teacher/ Literacy Clinic Specialist at Windsor Academy. This is her 22nd year with Columbus Public Schools. Robin loves to read, takes Tai Chi classes, and is very involved in church activities. She lives in Columbus, Ohio with her husband and two stepsons.